Most Extreme Jobs

Glen Downey

Series Editor
Jeffrey D. Wilhelm

Much thought, debate, and research went into choosing and ranking the 10 items in each book in this series. We realize that everyone has his or her own opinion of what is most significant, revolutionary, amazing, deadly, and so on. As you read, you may agree with our choices, or you may be surprised — and that's the way it should be!

Franklin Watts

an imprint of

SCHOLASTIC

www.scholastic.com/librarypublishing

A Rubicon book published in association with Scholastic Inc.

Rubicon © 2008 Rubicon Publishing Inc.
www.rubiconpublishing.com

Associate Publishers: Kim Koh, Miriam Bardswich
Project Editor: Amy Land
Editor: Bettina Fehrenbach
Creative Director: Jennifer Drew
Project Manager/Designer: Jeanette MacLean
Graphic Designer: Julie Whatman

The publisher gratefully acknowledges the following for permission to reprint copyrighted material in this book.

Every reasonable effort has been made to trace the owners of copyrighted material and to make due acknowledgment. Any errors or omissions drawn to our attention will be gladly rectified in future editions.

"Being a Forensic Psychologist" by Robert A. Kutner, Psy.D. May 8, 2007. Reprinted with permission.

"Siegfried and Roy Incident Underscores the Dangers of Exotic Pets" (excerpt). From The Humane Society of the United States, October 6, 2003. Reprinted with permission of The Humane Society of the United States.

"Hollywood's best stunt performers deserve to get an Oscar thrill" (excerpt) by Renée Graham. From The Boston Globe, June 28, 2005. Reprinted with permission of The Boston Globe.

"8,000 gather to honor firefighters' bravery" (excerpt) by Martin Kasindorf. From USA Today, November 6, 2006. Reprinted with permission.

Cover: Firefighter battles wildfire-© Gene Blevins/LA Daily News/Corbis

Library and Archives Canada Cataloguing in Publication

Downey, Glen R., 1969-
       The 10 most extreme jobs / Glen Downey.

Includes index.
ISBN 978-1-55448-536-9

       1. Readers (Elementary). 2. Readers—Professions.
I. Title. II. Title: Ten most extreme jobs.

PE1117.D6932 2007a   428.6   C2007-906694-1

1 2 3 4 5 6 7 8 9 10   10   17 16 15 14 13 12 11 10 09 08

Printed in Singapore

Contents

10

26

42

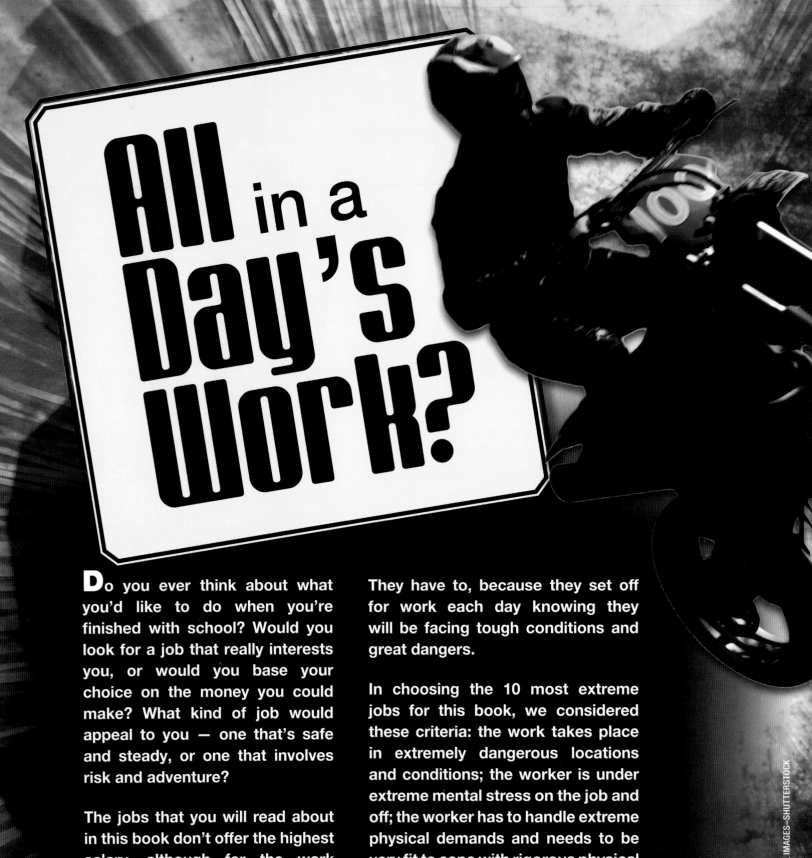

All in a Day's Work?

Do you ever think about what you'd like to do when you're finished with school? Would you look for a job that really interests you, or would you base your choice on the money you could make? What kind of job would appeal to you — one that's safe and steady, or one that involves risk and adventure?

The jobs that you will read about in this book don't offer the highest salary, although for the work these people do, we feel they should be paid big bucks! These are definitely not the regular nine-to-five desk jobs. People who hold these extreme jobs have a passion for what they are doing.

They have to, because they set off for work each day knowing they will be facing tough conditions and great dangers.

In choosing the 10 most extreme jobs for this book, we considered these criteria: the work takes place in extremely dangerous locations and conditions; the worker is under extreme mental stress on the job and off; the worker has to handle extreme physical demands and needs to be very fit to cope with rigorous physical conditions; and the person has to be very well trained in special skills to handle the job.

As you read the selections in this book, ask yourself:

Note: This book is about extreme jobs, which can be dangerous and should be done only by trained professionals.

WHICH IS THE MOST EXTREME JOB OF ALL?

A forensic psychologist testifies about a suspect's state of mind during a trial.

YCHOLOGIST

JOB DESCRIPTION: Using your knowledge of human behavior to help the court make a decision during a trial

WHAT'S SO EXTREME? Forensic psychologists put their lives at risk — especially when a suspect they deal with is emotionally unstable and likely to cause harm.

"Will the defendant please rise?" Forensic psychologists are very familiar with these words. "Forensic" refers to the application of scientific knowledge to help solve legal issues or criminal cases. In other words, forensic psychologists spend a lot of time in the courtroom.

Everything about this job is extreme. Forensic psychologists deal with cases that involve extreme emotional behavior and sometimes violence. They are faced with the strong emotions surrounding child custody battles. They witness the shocking results of a crime. They may even be exposed to the unpredictable behavior of those charged with brutal crimes.

No job in this book forces an individual to make more extremely difficult choices than this one does. And no other job leaves someone more open to severe consequences if a suspect is not happy with his or her evaluations or recommendations.

child custody: *legal right to raise a child*

FORENSIC PSYCHOLOGIST

JOB PREP

Of all the jobs in this book, this one is the most demanding in terms of education. A forensic psychologist must hold a 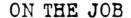doctorate in psychology. Then he or she needs years of practical experience, hundreds of hours of specialized training in forensic psychology, and the successful completion of an oral and written examination. Forensic psychologists must also devote themselves to a lifetime of academic training to keep up with new developments in their field.

Actor Morgan Freeman played a forensic psychologist in the 1997 film Kiss the Girls.

ON THE JOB

Forensic psychology deals with various fields of law. In civil cases, a forensic psychologist might be called in to determine whether or not someone has been harmed by an event. In cases involving workers' compensation, a forensic psychologist might be asked to describe how workplace stress could affect a person. In child custody battles, a forensic psychologist could be asked to decide whether a parent is fit to take care of the child. Forensic psychologists may visit maximum security prisons, psychiatric hospitals, courtrooms, and crime scenes when they are on duty.

---

doctorate: *highest degree awarded by a university*
civil: *relating to the rights of private citizens; not criminal law*
workers' compensation: *money paid for injury or stress suffered at work*

NO LIMITS!

Forensic psychologists make recommendations and decisions every day on the job. Psychologists hope that there won't be any undesirable personal consequences as a result. But what's worse is the terrible and heart-wrenching drama that they see, hear, and experience on a daily basis as part of their job. Also, trying to understand the criminal mind to find out why someone committed a crime can be a pretty stressful experience. Being responsible for labeling someone as mentally unstable, or taking a child away from an unfit parent, can be very emotionally draining.

? Find out what roles the judge, defense attorney, and defense psychologist play in a case involving a forensic psychologist. Why is it important for a forensic psychologist to be well prepared?

Quick Fact

When a suspect pleads insanity, a forensic psychologist has to determine whether the suspect is really mentally unstable. If the forensic psychologist believes the suspect is sane, then that testimony will be used against the suspect.

The Expert Says...

" Being a forensic psychologist is exciting because ... you never know what to expect! One day you may be asked by the court to determine whether or not a criminal is legally insane, and the next day you may be deciding who is the best parent in a child custody dispute. "

— Robert A. Kutner, Psy.D., forensic psychologist

10   9   8   7   6

Being a Forensic Psychologist

A personal account by
Robert A. Kutner, Psy.D.

What makes a forensic psychologist one of the 10 most extreme jobs? Well, you often get to work in a number of interesting, though anxiety provoking, settings. They include courtrooms, prisons, and governmental agencies such as the FBI (Federal Bureau of Investigation) and the CIA (Central Intelligence Agency). You may interact with psychopaths and serial killers. Your evaluation may help determine whether a suspect is deemed not guilty by reason of insanity.

Forensic psychologists work with individuals who present a variety of mental illnesses (e.g., schizophrenia, substance abuse, dementia) and have somehow come into contact with the law, either criminal or civil.

> **?** Research some of these illnesses. Why might people who suffer from these illnesses need a forensic psychologist to evaluate them?

Criminal cases may involve determining issues of ability to stand trial. For example, if an individual who is mentally handicapped commits a serious crime, he or she may not have the capacity to understand the court proceedings or participate in his or her defense. A person must possess sufficient intellectual ability to enter a plea at his or her initial arraignment.

psychopaths: *people with mental disorders that can cause them to commit violent acts*

deemed: *believed to be*

arraignment: *formal reading of criminal charges against a person*

Best Day on the Job

Testifying in a case where a mentally challenged client was declared mentally competent to testify against her offender based on the results of my evaluation.

competent: *able*

Worst Day on the Job

When a woman with borderline personality disorder destroyed my office because she thought a stuffed animal on my bookshelf was staring at her.

Take Note

Forensic psychologists don't necessarily deal with physical stress, but the emotional and mental stress they face is extreme and challenging. Aside from the numerous qualifications needed, their work often deals with some disturbing aspects of human nature. In addition, there's always the risk of violent revenge from a suspect. These reasons place this job at #10.
- What factors do you consider when making a decision? What was the best decision you've ever made? Explain your answers.

9 LION TAMER

LION TAMER—© STEPHANE CARDINALE/PEOPLE AVENUE/CORBIS

10

JOB DESCRIPTION: Train lions to perform difficult tricks to entertain the public

WHAT'S SO EXTREME? A lion tamer might end up as the lion's lunch.

Have you ever watched a lion perform in a circus? Did you think it might be cool to be the trainer of the lion?

You might want to think again — given that lions weigh hundreds of pounds, are unpredictable, have razor-sharp teeth, and can kill a human being in seconds!

Lion taming is one extreme job! The trainer is dealing with a wild animal that is used to being "King of the Jungle." The lion might not be too excited about performing tricks.

All lion tamers have to be extremely careful. If they are too timid, the lion will smell their fear and pounce on them. On the other hand, if the lion tamers are too aggressive, the lion will get angry and attack! Anyone interested in applying for this job?

 How do you feel about keeping wild animals in cages and training them to perform for human entertainment? Should this be made illegal? Give reasons for your answers.

Lion tamers perform acts with lions that they have trained from cubs. Do not try this trick at home with your own pet!

LION TAMER

Gunther Gebel-Williams once said, "Working closely with animals — training them, understanding them, and getting across their beauty and intelligence to the people — for me, that's the best life I can have."

JOB PREP

Lion taming cannot be studied in a school. It requires an apprenticeship and on-the-job training with a professional animal trainer. This is usually someone who has been in the business for years and can pass on his or her wisdom and skills. It's difficult these days to find a place that trains circus acts, but there is one in Vermont called Circus Smirkus. It offers a summer course that teaches circus skills to anyone between 10 and 20 years of age.

? Some people have a natural ability to communicate with animals (think of the famous Dog Whisperer, Cesar Millan). Do you think this is a skill that can be learned? Explain your answer.

ON THE JOB

Lion taming can take place at a zoo, although it is more common in a traveling circus. One of the most famous circus acts is Ringling Bros. and Barnum & Bailey Circus. Probably the most well-known lion tamer from this circus was Gunther Gebel-Williams.

apprenticeship: *time during which a person works for another in order to learn a trade*

NO LIMITS!

This extreme job demands total mental concentration. The tamer works closely with the animal at all times. He or she has to be confident and in control. Having an "off day" at work is not acceptable. Nor is misreading the signals from the animal. Do their job well, and they might just tame their lions to do tricks. Do it poorly, and they might end up in the hospital.

Quick Fact

The term "lion tamers" is loosely used to refer to people who tame other big cats such as tigers and cheetahs.

The Expert Says...

" They're predators, so who can really know what goes on in their minds? Even though they're raised in captivity and they love us, sometimes their natural instincts just take over. "

— Kay Rosaire, who runs Big Cat Encounter, a show near Sarasota, Florida

Say aaah! A lion's canine teeth can be as long as 2.5 inches!

10 **9** **8**

Siegfried & Roy Incident Underscores
THE DANGERS OF EXOTIC PETS

Big cats, whether they are tigers or lions, pose a threat to their tamers, as you will find out in this article (dated October 6, 2003) from the Humane Society of the United States.

The white tiger named Montecore was born in captivity and raised by humans. The seven-year-old animal had been performing on stage since he was six months old. Yet neither his upbringing nor his apparent "tameness" could have altered what happened on Friday night, October 3, at the Mirage in Las Vegas.

Montecore, a 600-pound white tiger ... attacked his longtime handler, Roy Horn of Siegfried & Roy, in a horrific incident that played out in front of a live audience. ...

Says Wayne Pacelle, a senior vice president for the HSUS [Humane Society of the U.S.] ... "When the best-trained and most-experienced handlers of big cats can be attacked and dragged around like rag dolls, it is plainly obvious that untrained private citizens should not keep big cats as pets." ...

"Tigers are hunters — predators armed with tools and instincts shaped by nature to be efficient and explosive killers," [Richard Farinato, director of HSUS Captive Wildlife Programs] adds. ...

After all, if it can happen to Roy Horn, it can happen to anyone.

Roy Horn (right) and Siegfried Fischbacher performed their famous Las Vegas show with white lions and tigers for decades. In 2003, Roy was brutally attacked by a white tiger. He has not fully recovered from his injuries.

Quick Fact

Many lion tamers use chairs to tame lions. Seems a little silly to use a chair, doesn't it? According to Dave Hoover, a lion tamer, "Lions are very single-minded. When you point the four legs of a chair at them, they get confused. They don't know where to look, and they lose their train of thought."

Take Note

This extreme job roars in at #9 on our list. It takes a truly special kind of person to be a lion tamer! And it takes years of training to get the lion to be comfortable with an audience and take instructions on stage.
- Do you think that lions and other big cats can really be tamed? What is another animal that would be difficult to tame? Explain your answers.

Jumping out of buildings is just one of the many crazy stunts performed by stunt doubles.

STUNT DOUBLE

JOB DESCRIPTION: Performing someone else's stunts

WHAT'S SO EXTREME? Stunt doubles risk their lives performing dangerous stunts, and big-name movie stars get all the recognition!

They are the movie scenes that draw gasps of amazement and cheers: The hero leaps out of a tall building ... just seconds before it explodes into flames! The heroine revs up her car and chases the crook ... her car flies over the crook's car and lands right in front of it!

Did you think your favorite movie stars pulled off these stunts? Sorry to disappoint you, but these daring actions were most likely performed by Hollywood stunt doubles — the men and women who perform the seemingly impossible, crazy scenes that scriptwriters dream up. Movie stars will not perform those scenes because of the dangers involved, or because they do not have the necessary skills. Call up the stunt doubles!

This is a pretty extreme job — it is dangerous, the demands are intense, and there is very little public recognition. The movie stars are the ones who get the fame, applause, and rewards for the Hollywood stunt double's work.

STUNT DOUBLE—© CORBIS SYGMA

HOLLYWOOD STUNT DOUBLE

In The Matrix Reloaded, *Carrie Anne Moss did some of her own driving for the close-up shots. Debbie Evans, one of the world's greatest motorcycle stunt doubles, did all of the dangerous scenes.*

JOB PREP

Years of training in a special field, working, and developing a solid reputation are how to get noticed as a stunt double. To be able to perform the highly risky stunts, stunt doubles need to be true experts in their field. A race-car driver might be brought in for car chases and car-racing scenes. A firefighter might be hired to escape from a burning building. A skilled pilot could be called on for flying or crashing a plane. If you don't have the skills, you won't get the job.

? Think about a film you have seen recently. Was there a scene in which a stunt double was likely required? Briefly describe the scene and explain how it could have been done.

Quick Fact

The famous highway chase scene from *The Matrix Reloaded* was filmed in Oakland, California, where many of the best stunt people work. The rest of the movie was filmed in Sydney, Australia.

ON THE JOB

Hollywood stunt doubles can work in some pretty extreme locations, like extreme heights (jumping out of a building), extreme depths (scuba diving underwater), and extreme heat (desert scenes) or cold (winter scenes). Whether in the air, on land, or in the water, they can also work at extreme rates of speed.

? Do you consider yourself a risk taker? Why or why not?

NO LIMITS!

This job requires great concentration, since many of the stunts call for incredible coordination and timing. And as stunts get more sophisticated, the stunt double's job gets even more demanding. Alisa Hensley is a popular stunt double who has stepped in for Cameron Diaz in *Charlie's Angels II* and Nicole Kidman in *The Interpreter*. She has escaped explosions, jumped out of buildings, and fought more than a dozen men at a time. Matt Anderson is a stunt double who has appeared in famous films like *The Italian Job* and *G.I. Jane*. He is a firearms expert, a certified skydiver, and a scuba diver, among other things.

Workers take apart the helicopter that crashed during the filming of The Twilight Zone *in 1982. Actor Vic Morrow and two small children were killed when a pilot lost control of his helicopter and crashed into them during a stunt.*

10   9   8   7   6

HOLLYWOOD'S BEST STUNT PERFORMERS DESERVE TO GET AN OSCAR THRILL

**An article from *The Boston Globe*
By Renée Graham, June 28, 2005**

... Frank Pierson, the academy's [Academy of Motion Picture Arts and Sciences] president, announced last week that its board of governors rejected a proposal to create a new Oscar category to honor stunt performers. As the academy is "more focused on reduction [lessening] than addition," Pierson said, "the board is simply not prepared to institute any new awards categories." ...

Filmmakers and actors ... supported the proposal submitted by several stunt performers' organizations for a best stunt coordinator category. A statement on the Stunts Unlimited website, representing stuntmen, coordinators, and action directors, laments stunt performers going "unnoticed and unrewarded" by the academy. ...

Those who are willing to leap from buildings, be set on fire, or maneuver careering cars through traffic during a high-speed chase — and do so to make some much-better-compensated famous face look good — deserve more than a shrug from the academy. ...

Hollywood understands just how important those amazing scenes are, yet when it's time to honor the people who plan and execute them, the academy is unwilling to acknowledge their irreplaceable contributions. If, as the Academy Awards like to trumpet every year, their ... night is about celebrating the creativity, the spirit, and especially the magic of the movie industry, then it's time for adequate and respectful recognition for some of their most unheralded magicians.

laments: *regrets; expresses sadness*
maneuver: *move in a different direction*
careering: *swerving at a high speed*

trumpet: *declare loudly*
unheralded: *unrecognized*

The Expert Says...

" I was being blown out of a trailer in a harness and actually landed on my coordinator instead ... My arm smacked into the ground and obliterated one of the ligaments. "

— Zoe Bell, stunt double, referring to her role as Uma Thurman's stunt double in *Kill Bill*

obliterated: *destroyed*

Take Note

The stunt double leaps into the #8 spot. He or she is placed in a great number of extreme situations and has to perform highly risky stunts while the film's stars get all the credit (and the big paychecks).

• Think of some of the dangerous stunts you have seen in movies. Do you feel stunt doubles should be given the same recognition as the stars? Why or why not?

5   4   3   2   1

James Whittaker was the first American male to reach the summit of Mount Everest on May 1, 1963. The first American female was Stacey Allison on September 29, 1988.

IDE

JOB DESCRIPTION: Guiding people up the highest mountain in the world

WHAT'S SO EXTREME? Mount Everest guides work on some of the most dangerous terrain in the world, plus they face the dangers of snow blindness and acute mountain sickness!

This job takes us to the peak of the world. Located between Nepal and China, Mount Everest is the world's highest mountain. Climbing this giant is no easy task. You have to be physically fit to endure the rigorous climb. You need equipment and supplies just to stay alive — tents, proper boots and clothing, tools, and food. And you have to be prepared for unpredictable weather.

Now imagine being an Everest guide — you are responsible for the safety of the people you are leading. And since they have paid you a big fee to be their guide, you want to make sure they succeed in reaching the summit. So, you have to balance the group's safety against their eagerness to "conquer" Everest. What a job!

Guides usually bring Sherpas along on the trip. "Sherpa" is a loose term used to refer to the native people of Nepal. Because they live in villages high in the Himalayas, Sherpas are excellent guides — they are very fit and know their way around the mountain.

Nothing about the job of an Everest guide is easy. When it comes to the most extreme jobs, this one leaves most of the others at base camp.

base camp: *area where guides and climbers prepare for their climb to the summit*

EVEREST GUIDE

As if climbers needed another reminder of the dangers of Everest — they may come across frozen bodies in places that are hard for rescuers to reach.

JOB PREP

To be an Everest guide, you need to be in excellent health. You have to be physically fit to climb the rocky and icy slopes while carrying heavy gear. You have to be trained to function well at heights of above 8,200 feet. Because there is less oxygen in the air at that height, some people become dizzy or even confused. It is very important that you have years of experience as a mountain climber so you really know the dangers and how to avoid them. And most importantly, you must have great leadership skills. If the climbers you are leading don't have faith in you as a leader and guide, accidents are bound to happen.

If you were hiring a guide for an Everest climb, what qualities would you be looking for?

ON THE JOB

You can't get a more extreme workplace than the top of the world! Aside from the location being extreme, the weather is extreme too. Temperatures can fall well below freezing. And watch out for avalanches! They can be deadly. Because climbers pay huge fees (about $65,000 per person) to reach the summit, guides are under tremendous pressure to make sure the climbers succeed.

NO LIMITS!

There is no room for error, either from yourself or from those whom you are guiding. A wrong move from one individual can injure many, especially when you're connected on the same line to other mountain climbers. Take a wrong step crossing the icefalls and you can fall thousands of feet to your death. What's even more extreme is that you can do everything correctly and still end up dead if you get caught in a vicious storm!

Some people have argued that Mount Everest has become "too commercial" with so many people climbing it. Why do you think these people are so concerned?

Quick Fact

Each year Everest grows 0.158 inches because the two tectonic plates of Asia and India are pressing against each other. That may not sound like a lot, but in 1,000 years Everest will have grown 13 feet.

The Expert Says...

"I've been to Everest eight times now, and it never ceases to amaze me that you are always, always facing the great unknown ...

— Todd Burleson, mountain guide

10 9 8 **7** 6

Mount Everest by the numbers...

Mount Everest is an extraordinary mountain. In the words of one mountain climber, "Everest has always represented nature at its most powerful, most awe-inspiring, most unconquerable." It's majestic, magical, and breathtaking. These are just a few reasons that people take a chance in climbing it. It's also dangerous, risky, and unforgiving, which may lead to serious injury and sometimes death. To get the big picture, read this list of extreme numbers.

29,035 Height in feet, making this magnificent mountain the highest in the world.

26,250 Height in feet at which most expeditions start using oxygen masks and tanks. With less oxygen, people don't think clearly, and at this level, quick thinking is necessary.

17,715 Height in feet where the base camp is located. This is where the guides and climbers prepare for their ascent to the summit.

250 Speed in mph that winds can reach at the peak of Mount Everest. Imagine withstanding winds this fierce as you're trying to climb!

186 Number of people killed trying to reach the summit of Everest.

15 Number of climbers killed in 1996, including famed guides Rob Hall and Scott Fischer. This was the highest number of deaths in a single year on Everest.

2 Number of months it takes to climb Mount Everest. A climbing team departs on March 31, treks to base camp April 4–23, begins ascent mid-May, and descends June 1.

Quick Fact

Scott Fischer was well known outside of being an Everest guide. He led a group to the summit of Everest in 1994 where they removed 5,000 pounds of accumulated garbage. He was praised for what he did for the environment.

Take Note

Everest guides climb into the #7 spot. Not only do they face extreme dangers working in an extreme location, these guides also have to make sure the people they are leading can safely reach the summit.
- If you were given the opportunity to climb Mount Everest, would you do it? Why or why not?

5   4   3   2   1

6 EXPLOSIVE ORDNAN

An EOD operator practices a routine procedure with the help of a robot. Check out the gear the operator has to wear for protection!

CE DISPOSAL OPERATOR

EOD OPERATOR–U.S NAVY/JOURNALIST SEAMAN JOE EBALO

JOB DESCRIPTION: Disable explosives

WHAT'S SO EXTREME? If Explosive Ordnance Disposal operators make a mistake, the bomb could explode right in front of them!

Nothing clears a building faster than a bomb scare. Imagine being the person who has to go into the building when everyone else has left! Imagine having to take apart the bomb so it can no longer explode. Nervous folks need not apply for this job. Nerves of steel, extreme concentration, and steady hands are key requirements.

Explosive Ordnance Disposal (EOD) operators deal with bombs on a regular basis. We're not talking about the ones that drop from the sky in a video game. We're referring to real bombs that explode and cause massive damage! EOD operators are called in when bombs are discovered. Then they are expected to dismantle them. Sound scary? You bet!

EOD operators wear protective gear, such as helmets, goggles, bulletproof vests, and gloves. With modern technology, the EOD operator can sometimes send a robot to do the job. The operator uses a remote control to give commands to the robot. However, very often, the EOD operator has to go up close and personally dismantle a bomb. That's when the training and the steady nerves come in handy!

EXPLOSIVE ORDNANCE DISPOSAL OPERATOR

JOB PREP

EOD operators train with the military before they enter the bomb disposal field. They then take courses where they learn how bombs are made, how to dismantle bombs, and how to react in bomb threat situations. In addition, because more sophisticated bombs are being created all the time, EOD operators have to constantly learn how to dismantle new and more challenging bombs.

? What are some other jobs where employees always have to keep up with new information?

ON THE JOB

EOD operators work all around the world. They seek out and destroy land mines in war zones. They handle unexploded devices from demolition sites in different cities. They help soldiers deal with an enemy who is armed with an explosive device. Wherever an important government official is going, an EOD operator must go first to check for bombs.

demolition: *destruction of old or unsafe buildings*

Quick Fact

EOD operators are important during a war. In the invasion of Normandy, France, during World War II, EOD operators struggled along the shore with soldiers to dismantle booby traps and land mines, all the while being shot at by the enemy.

NO LIMITS!

Although it's not often that EOD operators actually touch a bomb themselves, there are times when it's absolutely necessary. This is usually in big cities or densely populated areas. There is no room for chance, and sending in a robot could be too risky. One wrong move could cause death and injury to many people. To avoid this, EOD operators are sent in to disable the bomb.

? In a life-or-death situation, would you trust a robot to disable a bomb, or would you rather have an EOD operator do it? Why?

Quick Fact

Because of their knowledge of explosive devices, EOD operators are sometimes called in to examine the remains of a blast caused by a bomb.

The Expert Says...

" The Airmen of the 99th Airborne Explosive Ordnance Disposal ... are constantly in harm's way — from defusing bombs, disarming booby traps and improvised explosive devices, to jumping out of an aircraft from low altitudes. "

— Travis Edwards, Senior Airman, Nellis Air Force Base Public Affairs

10 9 8 7 **6**

Tools of the Trade

Here is a list of the tools EOD operators use to help them do their job.

Pigstick

A pigstick is a device that can fire a high-speed blast of water to break the circuitry of a bomb, making it harmless. It is a valuable tool for the EOD operator and requires minimal maintenance.

EOD Canine

Dogs can be very effective in sniffing out chemicals that are used to create an explosive device. The dog shown to the right, Quincy, was trained by the King County Sheriff's Department in Seattle, Washington, to find ammunition, firearms, bombs, and their various parts.

Bomb Disposal Robot

If you're not interested in getting too close to the suspicious package, and you're not willing to risk your EOD canine, then robots are the way to go. A bomb disposal robot, like the teleMAX shown to the right, can be successful in disarming explosive devices.

Explosives Vapor Detector

The Explosives Vapor Detector is used to trace and detect bombs on planes or in airports. It offers extremely fast and thorough detection when there is little time to do a complete search.

Take Note

Like forensic psychologists, EOD operators deal with extreme mental stress on the job. However, they, like lion tamers and stunt doubles, also face physical dangers. EOD operators risk not just their own lives, but also, if they make a mistake, the lives of other people in the area. These experts come in at #6 on the list.

• In your opinion, what kinds of personal qualities does an EOD operator require?

5   4   3   2   1

5 HOTSHOT

This Hotshot is trying to put out a forest fire in Corona, California.

JOB DESCRIPTION: Fighting the largest and deadliest forest fires

WHAT'S SO EXTREME? Everything about the job is extreme, from the expertise, or skill, needed to perform it to the dangers in carrying it out.

Ask kids what they want to be when they grow up, and at one point or another most kids will say the same thing: a firefighter. Why? Because in our society, firefighters are viewed as heroes.

Firefighting is a job that provides an incredible service to the community. It's a job where a person risks his or her life to save others from terrible situations.

But even in the world of firefighting, there are different levels of danger and intensity. This is especially true when a fire is at its largest and hottest, spreading throughout a forest and threatening towns in the area.

Hotshots are firefighters who fight large-scale forest fires. They often spend long periods of time in extreme conditions with very little backup.

Although being physically fit and having expert knowledge of firefighting equipment are absolutely essential, these qualities alone cannot fight the raging fires. However, if you can handle this kind of heat, you have what it takes to be a Hotshot.

HOTSHOT

Hotshot crews will often create backfires: they intentionally set controlled fires in an attempt to remove the fuel from the path of a raging forest fire.

JOB PREP

To become a Hotshot, you must first be trained as a firefighter. Through classroom instruction and practical training, Hotshots study firefighting techniques, fire prevention, emergency medical procedures, and first aid. They also learn how to use axes, chain saws, fire extinguishers, ladders, and rescue equipment. Even more important, Hotshots must have self-discipline, mental alertness, physical strength, and courage.

 Do you think the term Hotshot is an appropriate way to describe these elite firefighters? Explain.

ON THE JOB

Hotshots fight large-scale forest fires. Typically, this puts them in very dangerous locations. Many fires occur in states like California and Arizona because of the warm, dry weather. Forest fires in places like these can last for days and even weeks! Hotshots can sometimes be isolated for long periods of time, living in conditions without access to the comforts of warm beds, running water, and home-cooked meals.

NO LIMITS!

Let's face it — firefighting is extremely dangerous. Hotshot crews are surrounded by a fire's natural fuel on all sides. Because of this, they can't necessarily get relief from backup units if things start going badly. This puts them at significant risk when fighting fires. It's due to their fantastic conditioning and expertise that they are successful in this extreme line of work.

 What do you think would be the most significant dangers that a Hotshot would face on the job? Explain your answers.

Quick Fact

In order to qualify as a Hotshot for the Redding Interagency Hotshot Crew in California, you need to be able to travel close to three miles in 45 minutes carrying 45 pounds of equipment … and you need to be able to do this on the first day or you're sent home!

The Expert Says...

" … you're not just going on a hike in the woods with your lunch in your pack. It sounds like a good weekend — except that the woods are on fire. You have to be aware of danger all the time.

— John Markalunas, assistant superintendent of a Hotshot crew "

10   9   8   7   6

8,000 GATHER TO HONOR FIREFIGHTERS' BRAVERY

An article from **USA TODAY**
By Martin Kasindorf, November 6, 2006

DEVORE, California — High in the mountain pass that divides Southern California's fire-prone slopes from the Mojave Desert, the nation's firefighting community on Sunday somberly honored the five U.S. Forest Service firefighters fatally overrun last month in a wildfire.

The deaths of the Engine Company 57 crew in the 60-square-mile Esperanza fire were the greatest loss of firefighters in a wildfire since 14 died near Glenwood Springs, Colorado, in 1994, according to the National Interagency Fire Center. ...

The five were Capt. Mark Loutzenhiser, 43, of Idyllwild, the team's leader and a 21-year Forest Service veteran; Jason McKay, 27, of Phelan; Jess McLean, 27, of Beaumont; Daniel Hoover-Najera, 20, of San Jacinto; and Pablo Cerda, 23, of Fountain Valley. ...

"The fire changed direction so fast that there was nothing anyone could do," California Governor Arnold Schwarzenegger said. The men were "engulfed by windswept flames while trying to save someone's house. Firefighting ... is filled with true heroes who risk their lives in order to save others." ...

It took 2,000 firefighters aided by retardant-dropping planes five days to fully contain the Esperanza fire. It burned 40,200 acres — more than 60 square miles — and destroyed 34 homes. ...

U.S. Forest Service members enter the grounds for a memorial service honoring the five firefighters, November 5, 2006, in Devore, California.

engulfed: *surrounded by; enclosed*
retardant: *fire-resistant*

Take Note

Hotshots have earned the #5 spot. While EOD operators can sometimes count on robots for help, Hotshots are called in to help firefighters when a fire becomes too fierce and uncontrollable! And because forest fires can sometimes rage for weeks, Hotshots are usually there on the job, facing the dangers, for extended periods of time.

• Could you take a job that would separate you from your family and loved ones for an extended period of time? Why or why not?

5   4   3   2   1

Charles Crain, a reporter working for TIME magazine, takes notes during a gun battle on January 16, 2005 in Tal Afar, Iraq.

SPONDENT

REPORTER–CHRIS HONDROS/REPORTAGE/GETTY IMAGES

JOB DESCRIPTION: Covering news stories in the most dangerous places

WHAT'S SO EXTREME? War correspondents have to do their reporting while bombs are going off behind them and bullets are whizzing by.

With modern technology, the moment something important happens, the world knows about it — through television, the Internet, the radio, and even cell phones! We are always just a click away from up-to-the-minute news coverage.

In order to cover the latest news event in a war, war correspondents need to be where the news is happening. For years, war correspondents have been risking their lives in order to send back radio and written reports, photos, and film footage from the battlefield. Recently, embedded reporters have joined with military units on one side of the war. They have been able to get into the midst of a war zone, traveling along with the soldiers in their vehicles!

All journalists live by the motto of doing anything and everything to get a story — but does the extreme job of a war correspondent take it too far?

WAR CORRESPONDENT

JOB PREP

You can't walk into a major news station and tell them you want to be a war correspondent. First you need a university degree, preferably in journalism. Then you need several years of experience covering a variety of stories and assignments in tough locations. Once you have the experience, you are ready to become a war correspondent.

ON THE JOB

Whether you're in the middle of gunfire or near the blast of a suicide bomb, you can bet this job's location is extremely dangerous. It is difficult at times to understand exactly where you are, what the situation is, and what you are allowed to reveal about your location. You are on unfamiliar ground in a conflict zone for which you have received only some basic training.

War correspondents often reveal their location while giving the news. How can this be dangerous?

Reporter Michael Kelly was embedded with the U.S. Army's Third Infantry Division in 2003 when he was fired upon and killed by Iraqi rebel forces.

Quick Fact

War correspondents and embedded reporters face the same dangers in the war zone. Embedded reporters travel with the military force on one side of the war and are protected by them, but they are also the targets of the enemy. War correspondents often have to provide their own safety.

Do you think a war correspondent who works independently is more likely to give a fair and neutral account than a reporter embedded with one of the forces of a war? Why or why not?

NO LIMITS!

A war correspondent faces danger on the job. There are a number of terrible things that could happen while he or she is on assignment. Ambushes, bombings, booby traps, and extreme weather are just a few of the dangers. As well, there is no going home at the end of the day to recover. Any correspondent or reporter could spend weeks away from home while on assignment.

10   **9**   **8**   **7**   **6**

"Reporting from Taji ..."

Bob Woodruff is a journalist who was wounded by a roadside bomb in Iraq on January 29, 2006. Below is an article describing his experiences as an embedded reporter.

Bob Woodruff had seen some pretty unbelievable sights as a reporter.

He had seen the devastation left by Hurricane Katrina in his reporting from New Orleans, and the agony and despair that followed the deadly storm.

He had seen one of the worst natural disasters in modern memory with the Asian tsunami killing more than 225,000 people, including nearly 170,000 in Indonesia alone.

He had seen some horrifying things.

But on January 29, 2006, as Woodruff was traveling near the town of Taji in Iraq while taping a report inside an armored military vehicle, it was what he didn't see that changed his life.

The vehicle he was traveling in ran over and set off a bomb, and then immediately came under fire from rebel forces. Despite wearing body armor and helmets, both Woodruff and his camera operator, Doug Vogt, received head injuries. Woodruff's was so serious that part of his skull had to be removed during surgery in order to reduce swelling on the brain.

Bob Woodruff is prepared to be loaded onto a Mississippi Air National Guard C-17 to be transferred to the U.S. from the Ramstein Air Base in Germany.

Woodruff and Vogt were eventually transported to a hospital in Germany, and then to Bethesda, Maryland. Although Vogt was soon released from the hospital, Woodruff had to be placed in a drug-induced coma in order to help with his recovery.

Today, Woodruff continues to make progress on his road to recovery. He's unsure whether he'll return to war reporting, but he plans to report on stories about injured veterans returning home from war.

The Expert Says...

> Part of being a reporter is that you have to be somewhat addicted to adrenaline, particularly when you're working in foreign situations, covering wars and conflicts and civil strife.

— Bob Woodruff, embedded reporter

Take Note

War correspondents must deal with situations that are completely out of their control. They travel to conflict zones to report the news, even if it puts their lives in danger. That's why this job is #4 on our list.

- Imagine that as a war correspondent you found yourself in a situation where you could affect the combat that was going on. Would you do so? Why?

5   **4**   3   2   1

Combat search and rescue personnel retrieve an injured soldier. They risk their lives to save others.

RESCUE PERSONNEL

The situation is critical.

Imagine you're an air force pilot trapped behind enemy lines after your plane goes down. Although you were able to eject before the crash, you now have to figure out the best way to avoid detection by the enemy. There are also enemy forces that are doing everything possible to find you and prevent your escape. You can hold out for a while, but not for long.

The task before you seems scary — some would say hopeless. But although you find yourself in great danger, there's always someone else in the same situation.

The combat search and rescue (SAR) personnel you've just radioed have a tough job. Think about it … they have to enter enemy territory on purpose to rescue you!

"Brave" doesn't begin to describe the members of combat SAR personnel. These military teams are sent into combat to do three things: locate, communicate, and recover. These heroes risk their lives to save others in the face of danger.

COMBAT SEARCH AND RESCUE PERSONNEL

JOB PREP

Military and combat training is needed for combat SAR personnel. More often than not, SAR personnel receive instruction in the operation of military aircraft. Usually soldiers are rescued by helicopter, and the combat SAR personnel onboard are heavily armed in case of attack. They are always practicing dangerous missions so that they will be prepared for the real thing.

ON THE JOB

Combat SAR personnel are most often needed during times of war. They have to locate and recover their fellow soldiers who end up in dangerous locations. Whether they are in the air, on land, or at sea, these brave teams put themselves in danger by entering enemy territory. Their job is even more difficult because they cannot communicate with those soldiers for fear that the enemy will locate the soldiers first and capture them. Combat SAR personnel have to work very quickly and carefully so that they and those they are saving won't be detected by the enemy.

NO LIMITS!

Combat SAR personnel engage in an occupation that puts them in serious jeopardy. Once they're in enemy territory, they are targets. If they're not careful, they will certainly get injured, or maybe killed. These people sacrifice themselves to save others. Is there anything more dangerous than this?

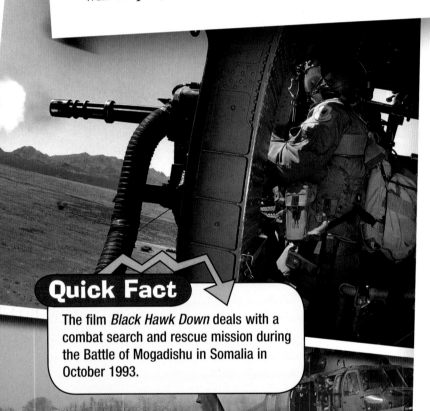

Quick Fact

The film *Black Hawk Down* deals with a combat search and rescue mission during the Battle of Mogadishu in Somalia in October 1993.

? Do you think a movie can ever really capture the true experiences of real-life events? Explain.

? What specific qualities do you think combat SAR personnel should have? Explain your answer.

10 **9** **8** **7** **6**

Behind Enemy Lines

Scott O'Grady is a former United States Air Force captain whose plane was shot down over Bosnia on June 2, 1995. The account below describes his six days in enemy territory and the heroic rescue by combat search and rescue personnel.

After Scott O'Grady's plane was shot down, he only had minutes to react. He quickly got rid of his parachute and rubbed dirt all over his face and ears. He put on green gloves so his skin wouldn't show. There were many times when the enemy was only a few feet away from him, but he stayed still and buried his face in the dirt.

 How do you think O'Grady felt when the enemy was only a few feet away?

The mission to save O'Grady was called TRAP, Tactical Recovery of Aircraft and Personnel. On the sixth day after O'Grady's disappearance, Captain Thomas Hanford finally received a radio call from the missing pilot — "I'm alive; help."

The rescue team had very little time to think. In the early morning hours of June 8, 51 marines, including 10 helicopter crew members, set out to find O'Grady. The combat SAR personnel made their way to the area where O'Grady's signal had come from. As they neared the spot, he set off a flare. The helicopter landed and O'Grady ran for his life toward the chopper. The SAR team grabbed onto him and the helicopter rose into the air.

The rescue mission was fired upon and almost taken down by the enemy. However, the pilot's expert flying and control of the chopper got the soldiers into the clear. Scott O'Grady was safe at last, thanks to the combat SAR personnel.

The Expert Says...

" They showed the nation and the world the best of our teamwork. Their mission made all Americans proud.

— Former U.S. President Bill Clinton speaking about the team that rescued Capt. Scott O'Grady from Bosnia

Take Note

War correspondents describe the details of war. Combat SAR personnel are part of the war. The intense mental and physical demands combined with the extreme danger of combat search and rescue missions are why this job comes in at #3 on our list.

• Compare the dangers faced by combat SAR personnel and Hotshots. Who has the more dangerous job? Explain your answer.

5   4   **3**   2   1

② TRIPLE AGENT

Tom Cruise plays Ethan Hunt, an agent, in the popular Mission Impossible movies.

JOB DESCRIPTION: Go undercover to gather and send secret information

WHAT'S SO EXTREME? Blow your cover, and you could lose your life!

A double agent is a person who pretends to work for Organization A, which sends him or her to spy on Organization B.

In fact, the double agent is working for Organization B, and is feeding Organization A false information about Organization B. At the same time, he or she is getting true secret information about Organization A and feeding it to Organization B.

Confused yet? Now here is what a triple agent does:

A triple agent actually works for Organization A. He or she gets hired by Organization B and pretends to be a double agent for Organization B. In fact, the triple agent provides Organization A with true secret information about Organization B.

Got that all figured out? One false step, and you blow your cover! And these organizations don't deal too kindly with secret agents who turn out to be traitors. Talk about extreme stress on the job!

Secret agents are sometimes described as moles. Why do you think they are given this nickname? Can you think of another animal that would make a good nickname for a triple agent?

TRIPLE AGENT

JOB PREP

Agencies such as the CIA (Central Intelligence Agency) select highly intelligent and well-educated people to be secret agents. They are trained to have absolute concentration and fearlessness in the face of danger. They also have to be experts at listening, lying, and in some cases, using lethal force. To be considered as an agent, you have to be at least 21 years old and no older than 37. You also need experience in law enforcement. You must pass the Treasury Enforcement Agent (TEA) written examination and have a complete background investigation, which includes in-depth interviews, a drug screening, and a medical examination. Speaking other languages fluently also helps.

ON THE JOB

Like any spy, a triple agent's work could take him or her anywhere in the world, depending on the organizations involved. Because triple agents pretend to be double agents, they might be forced to spend long periods of time behind enemy lines. This means the agents do a lot of acting to convince the enemy that they are on their side. Many times agents are unable to make contact with the organization for which they really work.

Do you think you have what it takes to be a secret agent? Could you pick up and leave at a moment's notice and not know where you're going or how long you'll be gone for? Explain your answers.

Sidney Reilly was a British agent who was said to be one of the inspirations for James Bond. Many suspect that he was either a double or triple agent.

NO LIMITS!

Triple agents always live under a cloud of suspicion. Having to pretend to be someone else to two or three different groups and having to juggle information among different parties make for extreme mental stress. Added to that is the danger of having their true identities revealed by the enemy. The result could be torture, imprisonment, or even death.

Quick Fact

A famous triple agent was Nikolai Skoblin. He gave information to the Russian All-Military Union, Joseph Stalin's secret police, and the German Gestapo during the 1930s. Stories conflict as to how he died, suggesting he was poisoned, tortured, or fled safely to another country and changed his identity.

The Expert Says...

" All warfare is based on deception. There is no place where espionage is not used. "

— Sun Tzu, Chinese military strategist and author of *The Art of War*

espionage: *using spies to obtain information*

8 7 6

Triple Agent—Not so SECRET

Want to be a secret agent? Read this list from the CIA about the myths surrounding the job and the agency.

Myth 1

You'll Never See Your Family and Friends Again.

The work we do may be secret, but that doesn't mean your life will be. The variety of CIA careers is similar to that of any major corporation. So … your friends and family will still be part of your life.

Myth 2

Everyone Drives a Sports Car with Machine Guns in the Tailpipes.

Car chases through the alleyways of a foreign city are common on TV, but they're not what a CIA career is about. And, they don't compare with the reality of being part of worldwide intelligence operations supporting a global mission.

Myth 3

You Have to be Superhuman in Every Way.

You don't have to know karate or look good in a tuxedo to work at the CIA. But you must possess a deep intellect, the ability to make good decisions, and a dedication to serving America through the collection of intelligence.

Myth 4

A Glamorous Lifestyle Awaits You.

Working at the CIA doesn't mean you'll be jet-setting around the globe, attending parties with billionaires, and showing off your tango skills. In reality, we depend on administrative managers and staff for our operational success, at home and abroad.

Myth 5

Hardly Anyone Ever Makes it Through the Background Check.

Because of our national security role, CIA applicants must meet specific qualifications — but, don't worry. …Your intellect, skills, experience, and desire to serve the nation are most important to us.

Take Note

The triple agent spins into the #2 spot. Combat search and rescue personnel risk their lives to defend their country. Triple agents do the same. However, a triple agent has the extreme job of juggling so many lies that his or her mind must be one tangled web!

- What does it take to be a CIA agent? Do some research and learn about the requirements for becoming an agent.

5   4   3   **2**   1

① ASTRONAUT

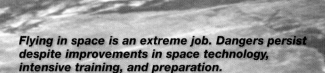

Flying in space is an extreme job. Dangers persist despite improvements in space technology, intensive training, and preparation.

WHAT'S SO EXTREME? You'll travel faster, fly higher, and see the world from a whole new point of view.

"We have liftoff!" This recognizable sentence describes the moments before an astronaut's amazing journey into space.

The term "astronaut" comes from Greek words meaning "sailor of the stars." It's an appropriate term since astronauts can be said to sail through space. Their mission might be to orbit Earth, land on the Moon, launch satellites, or dock with the International Space Station.

Whatever the mission, however, the life of an astronaut is definitely extreme. It takes years of training to have all of the necessary skills in order to pilot or even just ride on a ship worth hundreds of millions of dollars. And even then, an illness, injury, or change of plan might force you to watch the takeoff from the ground instead of experiencing the dream of a lifetime. In addition, the ride to space and back is incredibly dangerous. Any little piece that's loose on the ship could cause a massive explosion.

Extreme joys, extreme disappointments, extreme destinations, and extreme tragedies ...

Everything about being an astronaut is extreme.

orbit: *circle around a large object, held in position by its gravity*

ASTRONAUT AND EARTH—NASA

ASTRONAUT

JOB PREP

Astronauts need at least a bachelor's degree from a university. A degree in engineering and physics will get you noticed. Training can take years and is very intensive. Being physically fit is a must. Astronauts must swim at least 80 feet in their flight suits and running shoes, as well as tread water for 10 minutes. Candidates must get accustomed to weightlessness.

 Do you think you would enjoy being weightless? How do you think it would feel?

ON THE JOB

These days, trips to space usually last at least a week. During this time, astronauts are eating, sleeping, exercising, and working aboard the space shuttle. Astronauts can exit the shuttle to do a space walk, often to repair a damaged part or retrieve a satellite, among other things. Scientific research and experiments are also done in space to determine the long-term effects of living in space and for finding cures to diseases.

Quick Fact

Sally Ride became the first American woman to fly into space on June 18, 1983. She has created programs for young girls to gain an interest in science and math, and perhaps one day become interested in becoming astronauts.

NO LIMITS!

The dangers of the job are obvious. NASA (National Aeronautics and Space Administration) lost 14 astronauts on two space shuttle disasters.

Astronauts are thousands of miles from home, locked in a spaceship that protects them from a vacuum environment that could kill them in seconds. As well, astronauts have to brave reentry through Earth's atmosphere. Also, if they leave the shuttle to do a space walk, astronauts have to be suited up in a special spacesuit complete with an oxygen tank and weights to keep them somewhat grounded.

vacuum: *enclosed space with very little air*

One person who died during takeoff was Christa McAuliffe, a teacher from New Hampshire. Should teachers or other civilians be allowed to train as astronauts? Why or why not?

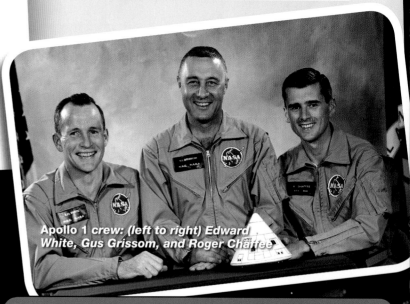

Apollo 1 crew: (left to right) Edward White, Gus Grissom, and Roger Chaffee

The Expert Says...

" I think we may have been misleading people into thinking that this is a routine operation, that it's just like getting on an airliner and going across the country and that it's safe. And it's not. "

— Sally Ride, astronaut, after the *Challenger* exploded in 1986

NASA

—Tragedies and Near Misses

With a history of almost 50 years, NASA has achieved a great deal in space. This has not come without a price, however, as we see in this chart below:

MISSION	DATE	PROBLEM	RESULT
Apollo 1	January 27, 1967	An oxygen fire occurs during the launchpad test.	Gus Grissom, Edward White, and Roger Chaffee are killed.
Apollo 13	April 13, 1970	An oxygen tank explosion damages the ship while flying to the moon.	Jim Lovell, Jack Swigert, and Fred Haise manage to guide the craft safely back to Earth.
Apollo-Soyuz Test Project	July 24, 1975	The landing capsule fills with toxic fumes after reentry.	Thomas Stafford, Vance Brand, and Deke Slayton manage to survive the incident, but stay in the hospital for two weeks under observation.
Space Shuttle Challenger	January 28, 1986	A problem with the O-ring seal in the solid rocket booster leads to the breaking apart of the shuttle 73 seconds after takeoff.	Michael Smith, Francis Scobee, Ronald McNair, Ellison Onizuka, Judith Resnik, Gregory Jarvis, and Christa McAuliffe (a teacher) are killed in the disaster.
Space Shuttle Columbia	February 1, 2003	*Columbia* breaks up during reentry as a result of damage sustained to its left wing during takeoff.	Rick Husband, William McCool, Michael Anderson, Ilan Ramon, Kalpana Chawla, Laurel Clark, and David Brown are killed in the disaster.

Space shuttle Columbia crew: (left to right) David Brown, Rick Husband, Laurel Clark, Kalpana Chawla, Michael Anderson, William McCool, and Ilan Ramon.

Take Note

When you consider all the factors that make a job extreme — danger, location, physical and psychological demands, and necessary qualifications — the job of an astronaut is simply the most extreme. That is why astronauts are #1 on our list.

• If you were given the opportunity to travel to space, would you accept it? Why or why not?

5 4 3 2 **1**

We Thought ...

Here are the criteria we used in ranking the 10 most extreme jobs.

The job:
- Is dangerous
- Involves substantial training
- Requires unique qualifications
- Is physically demanding
- Is psychologically demanding
- Occurs in risky locations
- Requires extreme concentration
- Calls for extensive travel
- Risks people's lives

What Do You Think?

1. Do you agree with our ranking? If you don't, try ranking them yourself. Justify your ranking with data from your own research and reasoning. You may refer to our criteria, or you may want to draw up your own list of criteria.

2. Here are three other extreme jobs that we considered but in the end did not include in our top 10 list: Alaskan king crab fisher, coal miner, and escape artist.
   - Find out more about them. Do you think they should have made our list? Give reasons for your response.
   - Are there other extreme jobs that you think should have made our list? Explain your choices.

Index